Positive Affirmations Business & Money Vision Board Clip Art Book for Men & Women: Empower Toolkit Series

Welcome to The Empower Toolkit Series: Positive Affirmations Business & Money Vision Board & Clip Art Book for Men, and Women! This edition has 250+ inspirational affirmation cards, images, and phrases designed for men and women.

This book is your creative playground, filled with:

- Inspiring images
- Affirmations
- Empowering phrases

Step into your power and manifest financial success with the Positive Affirmations Business & Money Vision Board Clip Art Book for Men and Women, part of the Empower Toolkit Series. This series features the Positive Affirmations Vision Board Clip Art Book, Positive Affirmations Vision Board Clip Art Book for Black Teen Girls, and Empower Vision Board Clip Art Book for Black Women. Packed with 250+ bold visuals, uplifting affirmations, phrases, and actionable content, this book is designed to help you create a clear path toward your goals. Whether you're building a vision board, journaling, or seeking daily inspiration, this clip art book gives you the tools to unlock your potential, embrace abundance, and achieve lasting success. Get ready to elevate your mindset and visualize the future you deserve with this essential resource for self-empowerment and growth!

How to Create a Vision Board: A Quick Guide

Materials Needed:

Poster board or corkboard

Magazines and printables

Scissors

Glue sticks or Mod Podge

Markers and pens

Stickers and decorative items

Personal photos

Tape or push pins (optional)

Steps to Create Your Vision Board:

Collect all the listed materials and set up a comfortable workspace.

Find Inspiring Images and Words:

Cut out or print images and words that represent your goals.

Prepare Your Base:

Arrange your images on the board before gluing or pinning them.

Affix Items to Your Board:

Glue or pin your images and words onto the board.

Add Personal Touches:

Write specific goals, affirmations, or quotes on the board.
Display Your Vision Board:

Place it in a spot where you'll see it daily.
Review and Update:

Regularly review and update your vision board as your goals evolve.
Conclusion:
A vision board helps visualize and manifest your dreams. With creativity and the right materials, you can create a motivating tool to keep your goals in focus. Start today and see your aspirations come to life!

My finances support the lifestyle of my dreams.

I am empowered to create the financial life I desire.

I make choices that align with financial independence.

I am free from the stress of money struggles.

I deserve to live a financially abundant life.

I attract opportunities that lead to financial freedom.

I have complete control over my financial future.

My income allows me to enjoy true freedom.

I live a life free from debt and financial worry.

I am financially free and secure.

Wealth Mindset

My mindset is focused on abundance and wealth.

I have a millionaire mindset.

I attract prosperity through positive thinking.

My thoughts create my financial reality.

I believe wealth flows to me easily.

I deserve to live a prosperous life.

I see opportunities for wealth all around me.

My wealth grows as my mindset evolves.

I think like a successful Entrepreneur.

I am open to limitless wealth and abundance.

Entrepreneurial Spirit

I AM A VISIONARY ENTREPRENEUR WITH LIMITLESS POTENTIAL.

MY IDEAS TURN INTO PROFITABLE VENTURES.

I AM CONFIDENT IN MY ENTREPRENEURIAL JOURNEY.

I LEAD MY BUSINESS TO SUCCESS WITH PASSION.

I TAKE CALCULATED RISKS THAT LEAD TO GROWTH.

MY ENTREPRENEURIAL SPIRIT DRIVES ME TOWARD GREATNESS.

I AM CONSTANTLY INNOVATING AND CREATING VALUE.

MY BUSINESS THRIVES BECAUSE OF MY VISION.

I ATTRACT OPPORTUNITIES THAT FUEL MY SUCCESS.

I AM UNSTOPPABLE IN PURSUING MY ENTREPRENEURIAL GOALS.

EARN EXTRA INCOME

PASSIVE INCOME

I AM OPEN TO NEW OPPORTUNITIES FOR WEALTH.

I CREATE MULTIPLE STREAMS OF INCOME WITH EASE.

MY INCOME SOURCES ARE DIVERSE AND GROWING.

I BUILD WEALTH FROM MULTIPLE AVENUES.

I ATTRACT PROFITABLE INCOME STREAMS EFFORTLESSLY.

MY FINANCIAL PORTFOLIO IS RICH AND VARIED.

I EXPAND MY INCOME SOURCES WITH CREATIVITY.

I MANAGE MY INCOME STREAMS WITH SKILL.

DIVERSIFYING MY INCOME LEADS TO FINANCIAL SECURITY.

I AM CONSTANTLY FINDING NEW WAYS TO GENERATE INCOME.

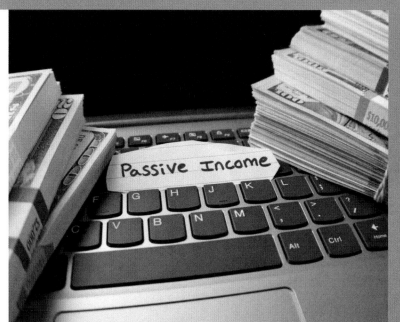

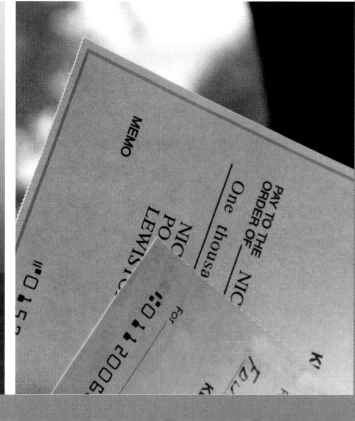

HUSTLE

HUSTLE

CREATE

CREATE

GET IT DONE

GET IT DONE

FABULOUS

FABULOUS

Goal Setting

- **S** specific
- **M** measurable
- **A** attainable
- **R** relevant
- **T** time-bound

I set clear and achievable financial goals.

My goals align with my values.

I achieve every financial goal I set.

I stay focused on my financial targets.

I am committed to reaching my goals.

I celebrate every milestone on my journey.

I track my progress toward financial success.

I am disciplined in pursuing my financial goals.

My goals guide my financial decisions.

I turn my goals into reality.

I make smart investments that grow my wealth.

My assets are valuable and continually increasing.

I build wealth through thoughtful asset allocation.

I am confident in my investment choices.

I am strategic in building long-term assets.

My investments bring financial security.

I create wealth by growing my assets.

My portfolio is diverse and profitable.

I am a savvy investor with a wealth-building mindset.

I leverage my assets for financial success.

DEBT FREE LIVING

I am debt-free and financially empowered.

I release the burden of debt.

My financial decisions lead to freedom.

I prioritize paying off my debts quickly.

I am proud to be debt-free.

I manage my finances responsibly.

I make choices that keep me debt-free.

My financial freedom grows daily.

I am in control of my money.

Living debt-free brings me peace and joy.

Networking and Building Connections

I attract valuable and supportive connections.

My network is filled with influential and inspiring people.

I build meaningful relationships that fuel my success.

I am surrounded by people who uplift and encourage me.

My connections open doors to new opportunities.

I network with confidence and authenticity.

My circle is rich with wisdom and guidance.

I form partnerships that lead to success.

I connect with people who share my vision.

I thrive in a network of growth-minded individuals.

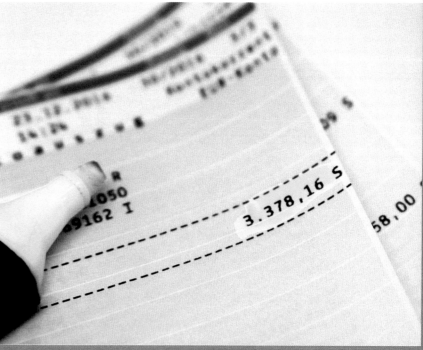

I AM DISCIPLINED IN SAVING FOR MY FUTURE.	MY SAVINGS GROW CONSISTENTLY AND SECURELY.
I PRIORITIZE SAVING AND MANAGING MY FINANCES RESPONSIBLY.	I BUILD WEALTH THROUGH CONSISTENT SAVINGS HABITS.
I AM FOCUSED ON ACHIEVING MY SAVINGS GOALS.	I SAVE DILIGENTLY AND LIVE BELOW MY MEANS.
I AM PREPARED FOR FINANCIAL EMERGENCIES.	MY FINANCIAL DISCIPLINE LEADS TO STABILITY AND PEACE.
I SAVE WITH PURPOSE AND INTENTION.	MY SAVINGS HABITS BUILD LASTING FINANCIAL SECURITY.

MY LEGACY IS ONE OF ABUNDANCE AND WISDOM.	I BUILD WEALTH THAT BENEFITS FUTURE GENERATIONS
I AM CREATING A LASTING IMPACT THROUGH MY FINANCIAL CHOICES.	MY LEGACY REFLECTS MY VALUES AND ASPIRATIONS.
I PREPARE FUTURE GENERATIONS FOR FINANCIAL SUCCESS.	I PASS ON KNOWLEDGE, WEALTH, AND OPPORTUNITIES.
MY LEGACY IS ROOTED IN PROSPERITY AND GROWTH.	I MAKE DECISIONS THAT SECURE MY FAMILY'S FUTURE.
I LEAVE BEHIND A POWERFUL FINANCIAL LEGACY.	MY WEALTH BUILDS A LASTING FOUNDATION FOR THOSE WHO FOLLOW.

Leaving a Legacy

777

Date _____

Pay to the
Order of _____ $ [   ]

_____ Dollars

memo _____   _____

⑆000000000⑆ 000000000000⑆ 0000

1000

_____ 20____

Pay to the
Order of _____ $ _____

_____ *Dollars* 🔒 Security features are included. Details on back.

For _____   _____

⑆111111111⑆ 222222222⑆ 1000

0001

Date _____ 20 _____

PAY TO THE
ORDER OF _____ $ [   ]

_____ DOLLARS 🔒 Security Features Details on Back

For _____   _____

⑆005552222⑆ ⑆005552222222⑆ 0001

DATE _____

PAY TO THE
ORDER OF _____ $ _____

_____ DOLLARS

MEMO _____ _____

0001

Date _____ 20 ____

PAY TO THE
ORDER OF _____ $ [   ]

_____ DOLLARS 🔒 Security Features Details on Back

For _____ _____

⑆005552222⑆ ⑆005552222222⑈ 0001

0001

Date _____ 20 ____

PAY TO THE
ORDER OF _____ $ [   ]

_____ DOLLARS 🔒 Security Features Details on Back

For _____ _____

⑆005552222⑆ ⑆005552222222⑈ 0001

NEXT EXIT

RESILIENCE

STRENGTH

OVERCOME BARRIERS

POSSIBLE

I FACE FINANCIAL CHALLENGES WITH STRENGTH AND COURAGE.	EVERY SETBACK IS AN OPPORTUNITY FOR GROWTH.
I OVERCOME FINANCIAL OBSTACLES WITH RESILIENCE.	MY FINANCIAL CHALLENGES DO NOT DEFINE ME.
I AM CAPABLE OF TURNING CHALLENGES INTO VICTORIES.	I LEARN AND GROW THROUGH FINANCIAL HARDSHIPS.
I RISE ABOVE FINANCIAL STRUGGLES WITH DETERMINATION.	I TURN FINANCIAL CHALLENGES INTO STEPPING STONES FOR SUCCESS.
I FIND SOLUTIONS TO EVERY FINANCIAL PROBLEM.	I CONQUER FINANCIAL HURDLES WITH GRACE AND CONFIDENCE.

Financial Literacy and Education

I MAKE INFORMED AND EDUCATED FINANCIAL DECISIONS.

I AM COMMITTED TO INCREASING MY FINANCIAL KNOWLEDGE.

FINANCIAL LITERACY IS MY KEY TO SUCCESS.

I SEEK OUT OPPORTUNITIES TO LEARN ABOUT MONEY.

I AM KNOWLEDGEABLE ABOUT MANAGING AND GROWING MY WEALTH.

I AM FINANCIALLY EMPOWERED THROUGH EDUCATION.

I EMBRACE CONTINUOUS LEARNING ABOUT FINANCES.

I AM A LIFELONG STUDENT OF FINANCIAL SUCCESS.

I VALUE THE POWER OF FINANCIAL EDUCATION.

MY FINANCIAL LITERACY OPENS DOORS TO WEALTH AND ABUNDANCE.

Made in the USA
Middletown, DE
13 December 2024